Tom Anderson has spent many years reading and studying authors of fiction from the Eighteenth and early Nineteenth centuries. It could truthfully be said that, outside of the main academic centres of learning, he is now a leading authority on this area.

Tom's latest area of research is into the sensibility novels, especially *The Man of Feeling, a novel of sentiment* published in 1771, written by Scottish author Henry Mackenzie

A GUIDE TO GOTHIC HORROR

Tom Anderson

A GUIDE TO GOTHIC HORROR

EMMA
STERN
PUBLISHING

An Emma Stern Publication

Copyright © Tom Anderson **2016**

The right of Tom Anderson to be identified as author of this work
has been asserted in accordance with sections 77 and 78 of the
Copyright, Designs and Patents Act 1988.

ISBN: 978-1-911224-18-1

Published in 2016

Emma Stern Publishing
107 Fleet Street
London
EC4A 2AB

www.emmastern.com
www.facebook.com/emmasternpublishing
Email: editorial@emmastern.com
Email: marketing@emmastern.com

Printed in Great Britain

All literature is in some way a reflection of life. Even when the fiction seems far removed from reality, we are learning something about the interests of writers and readers. Yet literature is not just a simple reflection. Reading novels affects the way we see reality. The story affects our emotions and the ways in which we think. At the same time, our own emotions and thoughts are brought to our reading. It is a two-way process.

In literature, as in life, there is always a reason for something. Nothing can escape the laws of cause and effect. So, by the middle of the C18 there was a turning away from the Classicism that was the dominant mode of literature. Classicism, with its control of emotions, had itself been a reaction to the religious emotions and fanaticism of the C17. Those emotions and that fanaticism had led to a terrible Civil War. Classicism, with its stress on control and lack of emotionalism, was partly a desire never to return to a period of upset in society. In this there was success: there was a period mainly of peace in Britain.

However, it is never possible for things to stand still. Actions lead to reactions. People soon forget. New generations are born. So, by the middle of the C 18, the civil wars and the emotionalism of the C 17 were a dim memory. Emotions and enthusiasm could not be contained for all time. The Gothic Horror novel, which emerged in the middle of the C18, was part of a wider movement away from Classicism toward Romanticism.

This movement called Romanticism did not begin with Wordsworth and Coleridge, though their joint publication of The Lyrical Ballads in 1798 was 'a landmark of English Romanticism and the beginning of a new age. 'The term 'Romantic 'is one that covers a very wide range of subjects. It was political, social and literary. In politics it was inspired by revolutions in America against Britain in 1776, and the revolution in France in 1789. Socially it was a movement that put the individual higher than group, and put stress on individual sensibility. In literary terms the Romantic Movement included many elements.

The Romantic Movement itself did not emerge and then not develop. It was also in a state of continual change. Among these elements in the beginning, however, there was a renewed interest in Nature (the Classical or Augustan period was mainly confined to towns and cities such as London and Edinburgh); a willingness to be enthusiastic; a support for what were then seen as progressive movements. At the same time there was an interest in the past. Especially in the medieval period, or the Middle Ages. The medieval period was a few centuries of religious Christian faith. It was a time when people were interested in religious mysteries.

The early period of Romanticism always had within it this element of looking back to the past. Not to a golden age, perhaps, but to a time when another world, a world of mystery, existed side by side with the real world. For people in the medieval period, the Middle Ages, it was possible to believe in angels and in devils. In the preface to The Castle of Otranto, Horace Walpole pretended that the story was a translation, by William Marshal, from the work of an Italian author called Onuphrio Muralto. It was, he said, 'a narrative of the most improbable and absurd adventures. '

The word Gothic referred originally to this medieval period, to the Germanic tribe known as the Goths. They were wild and savage, and had not been converted to Christianity. They were barbarians. This was everything that the classical scholars of the C17 and C18 feared most - uncontrolled emotions leading to civil disorder. It was necessary for leaders to be civilised so that they could control and subdue the barbarians within society.

These barbarians were peasants without education, the Irish with a different religion, and even the followers of the Stuarts who wanted the return of a catholic king.

It is possible to keep the lid on a boiling pot for only a short time. Soon, the lid will blow off. By the middle of the C18 the emotional nature of people, never far from the surface, was struggling to re-emerge. This element was what Samuel Johnson called 'This wild strain of imagination. '

There was a fascination with horror and imagination which the Gothic novel both reflected and fed. There is always a strong and powerful suggestion of terror. There is a castle. It is dark and isolated and medieval. It seems as if light has never penetrated to the centre of this castle. There is The Castle of Otranto (Walpole), of Udolpho (Ann Radcliffe) and Jane Austen's Northanger Abbey, which, despite the name, is in fact a large castle-like house owned by the Tilney family. Such castles, with their battlements, dark corridors, with light and shadow like ancient patterns, appealed to people who were fed up with the austerities of Classicism. Castles and mysteries appealed to the new Romantic rebels, because in all rebellions there is both a looking forward and a looking back. The Gothic novel satisfied curiosity in a barbaric past, a time of mysteries and fear.

Yet it was a fear that could be safely indulged. It was escapism without danger. Catherine Morland and her friend Isabella Thorpe can read and send shivers down their spines, but as they close a novel they know that they are not really in danger. It is fantasy without fear.

Other elements within the Gothic novels, which also account for their popularity, are connected with these fears. There are often abductions, sometimes torture. There is also the suggestion and fear of rape. The foreign settings assist here. Otranto and Udolpho are set in Italy, still in the C18 a place known to be Catholic, backward, and fearful. One novel is actually titled The Italian. This was written by Ann Radcliffe. The novel, Radcliffe's final book, is set in Italy. The hero, Vivaldi, and the heroine, Elena, are terrorised. There is an evil monk, called Schedoni. Vivaldi's own family want to see him dead. Innocent people, male and female, are in peril. This is a recurring element of much fiction, as well as of films. The Gothic heroine is the medieval 'damsel in distress ', the Lady of Shalott pale and doomed, Keats' La Belle Dame Sans Merci, alone and palely loitering, or the Julia Roberts character in The Pelican Brief and many another movie. It is the ancient struggle between good and evil.

This theme is best presented, whether in stories or in films, when the heroic people have faults, and the villains have some redeeming features. In real life nobody is wholly good and innocent and there are very few people who are entirely evil. In the Gothic genre, however, the two opposing sides are presented as very good or very evil. The heroine, often without proper help (Elena is an orphan; Catherine Morland is alone at Northanger Abbey, not supervised even by Mrs Allen) is likely to be imprisoned, raped, or savagely attacked in other ways. There is depravity about, especially among foreigners such as Italians. There may be a suggestion of incest, as in The Castle of Otranto. Or in The Monk, by M. G. Lewis, often known as 'Monk 'Lewis, where Ambrosio commits incest with a girl without knowing she is his sister.

These are all ancient sexual fears - rape and incest are among the greatest of taboos - and they appealed to the readers of the early Gothic novels. There was a class of females from the upper and middle classes who had received some education but were not allowed to work. They could not spend all their leisure time in gossip and embroidery. So they were among the most avid readers of Gothic novels. The elements of terror brought some excitement into their otherwise limited worlds. Ann Radcliffe capitalised on this. She was a woman writer writing for women. These were a kind of seduction novel. They presented the happy ending of love and marriage as the way for a young woman to be safe from fears and longings. This too was a form of escapism.

Along with the elements of sexual fear and terror, there was also the element of the supernatural. There might always in the end be a natural explanation for what seemed mysteries and supernatural, but the fear and terror came in the construction of the fear and attraction of the supernatural. As today we go to watch a film in darkness in order to be terrified (just as we go on frightening rides at fun fairs) so the readers of Gothic novels paid money to be frightened. The way in which the scene is set in these novels is very well done. There is darkness, broken only occasionally by moonlight or candles; there is mystery, when rooms are kept locked; owls screech and bats fly; there are footsteps in corridors; monks pass by, their faces hidden. And always there is the fear of death. There are gravestones and vaults. The remembrance of a dead wife still haunts the castle. There are secret letters.

A typical example is found in The Romance of the Forest. Adeline, the young heroine, has found a scrap of paper in a hidden room in a ruined abbey. This paper tells a story of imprisonment and suffering in that abbey. All these elements combine to produce wonder, fear and superstition. Adeline is fearful. Her fear is aroused by the words,

'Last night! last night! O scene of horror!'

she shudders with fear, 'yet curiosity prompted her to proceed.' She reads that there has been a horrid deed, the very worst, for there has been a murder. 'The idea thrilled her with horror.' In the same fashion, we pay to go on the Ghost Train. We are afraid. We dare not look. Yet we are compelled to peep, even when we know that we will be terrified.

One theme of Romanticism was the idea that individuals matter. There was a belief that people are born innocent and are then spoiled or depraved by society. Rousseau, among others, peddled this notion. The C18 saw a great deal of interest in the unspoiled savage. The term given this was 'the noble savage '. People are born innocent, they come, as Wordsworth writes, 'trailing clouds of glory ' Aphra Behn expresses this interest in the primitive in her novel Oroonoko, possibly the first expression in fiction of the 'the noble savage', and certainly the first to include people of African tribal origin.

Terror holds its own fascinations. It also has within itself certain dangers. The Gothic novel has always been perceived as mainly a form of writing intended for women, and in most cases produced by women. In this sense it is ranked alongside the thousands of stories published by Harlequin/Mills & Boon. The Castle of Otranto and The Mysteries of Udolpho were both originally advertised as 'romances '. The genre known as Gothic horror is best seen as a strand within Romanticism. It is situated within the early phase of the Romantic Movement. What we might call the medieval or looking-back period. We cannot imagine Wordsworth being influenced or frightened by the supernatural. Yet his contemporaries - Byron, Dr. Polidori and Mary Shelley - certainly were, and out of their interest came Frankenstein. The very mention of Frankenstein proves that Mary Shelley wrote what is in certain respects the best of the Gothic genre, just as Jane Austen's Northanger Abbey is a witty and clever subversion of the form.

Out of this intense interest came Frankenstein, or the Modern Prometheus. As well as Frankenstein, there came, also, The Vampyre by John Polidori, the doctor friend of Byron and the Shelleys.

What, we have to ask ourselves, accounts for the continuing interest and potency over two centuries of the Frankenstein myth and its regular adaptation to other media?

Things do not happen by chance. There are always reasons, always causes. Events cannot happen in a vacuum. It is true that Frankenstein has been a potent myth for almost two centuries. This is because Mary Shelley put into her novel a number of elements that are timeless. Elements that refer to our deepest wishes and our deepest fears. In a rational age, where religion is in decline, people think they have got rid of superstition. People who live in the present, feeding on materialism, think they have abolished the past. They are trying to fool themselves. Those ancient fears and superstitions have a way of coming back. They may return in our dreams. Or in powerful novels such as that written by young Mary Shelley. What started as a novel, has been adapted to other media, most powerfully - and certainly most popularly into cinema. Both consciously and unconsciously, Mary Shelley referred to the deepest parts of human nature.

It could be said that in an age of science and industrialism there is no need for myths. Rational people are not swayed by religion, ancient beliefs, or myths. In fact, the opposite is true. As society becomes more industrialised and more secular, so there is a return to ancient myths. This may not be conscious but may be more powerful for being unconscious in its origins. In 1950 Octavio Paz wrote: 'contemporary man has rationalised the myths but he has not been able to destroy them.' The truth is, myths cannot be destroyed. If they are thrown out of the door, they will return through the open window; they will return in disguise.

We are able to approach Mary Shelley's novel first through its sub-title, The Modern Prometheus. The story of Prometheus is pre-Christian. According to Greek myths and legends, it was Prometheus who stole fire from Heaven, and for this he was punished eternally. Mary Shelley knew the Prometheus story; Percy Shelley, her husband, himself wrote poems about him. Prometheus has for two centuries been the figure that attracts rebels - rebels such as Shelley himself and his friend Lord Byron.

Mary Shelley herself describes her novel as her 'tiresome unlucky ghost story '. But she was well aware, as she signals in the sub-title, that this was more than just a ghost story. The sources for the tale go deeper than a holiday game or a challenge during a visit to Switzerland. When Mary at last found the idea for her story - from a dream that terrified her - she declared: 'I have found it! What terrified me will terrify them.' Ghost stories can be silly or powerful. There are no such things as ghosts. Yet these stories persist even into the early C21. Ghost stories fulfil a need. They tap into the world of the unconscious mind. And the same is true of this novel of Frankenstein and his creation. It is an expression of unconscious repressed forces.

Part of the story's appeal and power lies in the fact that it can be read in different ways. Readers approach it with different views and perspectives. It speaks to us in the second decade of the C21 as much as it did to the first part of the C19. These different perspectives are political, literary and psychological. At deeper levels they are to do with religion. Life and death, creation and destruction, are all at the heart of the Frankenstein myth. And the novel is able to appeal to different cultures, different ages, but it also appeals to us in different ways at different times. It speaks to different parts of our human nature.

Frankenstein is a phenomenon of popular culture because it has successfully tapped into the centre of western feeling and imagination. It has also permeated other, non-Western cultures because of the spread of films and TV to all parts of the world.

Prometheus, in Greek mythology, made a man out of clay and stole fire from Heaven to give the clay creature life. Prometheus gave Man knowledge, and the power to create. For his acts he was punished by Zeus, king of the gods, by being chained to a rock. Each day a vulture came to tear at his liver. Frankenstein is a modern Prometheus. He seeks to create a living man. Out of the parts of several dead bodies, he makes his creature, and then seeks the spirit of life in the electricity of a thunderstorm. Like Prometheus, Frankenstein is playing at being God. This is the worst rebellion. This is the worst form of Pride. 'Pride goes before destruction, and a haughty spirit before a fall.' Of the deadly sins, pride is the deadliest and must always be punished. Like Prometheus, Victor Frankenstein is guilty of Pride on a cosmic scale.

Yet these references to Prometheus are not enough to explain the potency of the Frankenstein story. There are other mythic elements that go deep into the human Unconscious. Mary Shelley was fully aware of these elements too. Older even than the Prometheus myth, is the Judaic myth - which has come through to Christianity and to Islam - of Creation. In the beginning, God made the world, and he created the first Man. And out of that Man, he made Woman. For millions of people, Christian and Muslim alike, this is not a myth at all, but a literally true account of the beginning of the world. Many deny the theory of Evolution put forward in 1859 by Charles Darwin. Whether we believe the story in Genesis as fact or myth does not alter the fact that it has a powerful and elemental attraction. Everybody wonders about the origin of life on earth. We all marvel when a baby is conceived, and later when it is born.

And we all feel both fear and attraction for anyone who seeks to play God by creating life. This novel appeals to the twin emotions of fear and attraction.

Mary Shelley was a part of the Romantic Movement. She was indeed at its very centre, along with Shelley and Byron. The Romantics were strongly influenced by John Milton and his long poem called Paradise Lost. In this poem, Milton tells the story of how Adam and Eve disobeyed God by eating of the Tree of Knowledge. The poem is about the expulsion of Man and Woman from the Garden of Eden. It is about the loss of innocence, the loss of Paradise. It is the end of the golden age. This story is central to the three monotheistic religions of Judaism, Christianity and Islam. Thus, its re-creation in the form of a modern novel touches on the beliefs of many people, and taps into conscious and unconscious fears and memories.

Mary Shelley admits this clearly by quoting John Milton's Paradise Lost at the beginning of her 1831 edition, even before the dedication to her father, William Godwin. So here again Mary Shelley is seen to be tapping into powerful buried fears and concerns. Why does God give us life, if we are to die? Why does Victor Frankenstein create his being, only to abandon him because he is perceived to be a monster? Surely, the creator has parental responsibilities toward the one created. A part of the whole myth is the fear of being abandoned in an alien universe. We are born only to die. It all seems to be without sense and meaning, especially to those who, in modern centuries, lack religious faith and belief.

Mary Shelley understood the elements that went into her story. Yet there was, as always, an element of luck. She first published in 1818. This was the time when educated people were being most influenced by science. And it was science allied to great changes on the political scene. The scientific discoveries of the C17 and C18 had been used for the Industrial revolution after 1760. By 1818 the industrial revolution in England was at full power. Society was changing fast. New towns and cities were being developed. The world was changing faster than ever before. Change bewilders people. It is at such times of change that people return to old fears and superstitions. This also explains, in part at least, the potency of the Frankenstein myth.

Victor Frankenstein is a chemist. He has a 'student's thirst for knowledge '. He is attracted by alchemy. Alchemists, such as Paracelsus, searched for two things: the philosopher's stone that turned base metal into gold; and the elixir of life, that could keep off the approach of death. After meeting Dr Waldman, in chapter 2 of the novel, Victor returns home and his 'first care was to procure 'the works of Agrippa, as recommended by Waldman, 'and afterwards of Paracelsus and Albertus Magnus', two alchemists. He studies the 'wild fancies 'of these writers with 'delight.' His aim, as he states, is to 'banish disease from the human frame, and render man invulnerable to any but a violent death.' The desire to defeat Death is as old as Man on earth. It is found in ancient times, in the Middle Ages, and in modern times in such things as transplantation of bodily organs. By letting this be a desire of her hero, Mary Shelley was again tapping into an ancient desire, and this explains too the potency and lasting appeal of the novel.

There is, also, in this novel another myth that is ancient and yet very modern. This centres round the existence of an invisible power - electricity. When Victor Frankenstein was five years old he witnessed 'a most violent thunderstorm.' He later learns from a visitor to the house all about electricity. In 1818 this was a new power, invisible and dangerous. It held the popular imagination in its grip. Such people as Franz Anton Mesmer, a hypnotist, claimed that his powers came from electricity. This was a fraudulent claim but many believed it. People want to believe. It is unbelief that is unnatural. Frankenstein was able to use the power of electricity to put life into a creature made up from parts of corpses. 'To unfold to the world the deepest mysteries of creation. '

People do not understand science or scientists. So, like primitive people in all ages and all continents, they ascribe what they do not understand to the powers of magic. Like Professor Waldman in the novel, like Dr Faustus, like Prometheus, Frankenstein wishes to 'penetrate the recesses of nature.' He is a modern Satan. He is the first of a long line of mad scientists 'grappling with a palpable enemy.' Once he has listened to and learned from Waldman, Frankenstein loses his prejudices against modern chemists. He wishes to apply science to 'the solid advantage of mankind. 'These could be the words of any Victorian reformer. Yet the Industrial Revolution turned out to be a monster.

This helps too to explain why the Frankenstein myth was powerful in the C19. It was widely believed or hoped that industrial society would lead to better people and more freedom. In the words of Professor Waldman to Victor Frankenstein, it would be 'the greatest improvement' that has been or can be made. Mary Shelley's novel fitted in well with early Victorian optimism, with ideas of improvement and reform. The spirit of Science was abroad.

Industrialism was allied to Romanticism and Liberalism. Both were optimistic movements that grew out of the same ideas that had brought about the

French Revolution of 1789. Man was capable of improvement. Human nature could rise above what was base. Poets and politicians could also create. Romanticism and Liberalism were secular forces. If human beings like Frankenstein were capable of creation, there was no need of God. Deep fears were being awakened by science. These fears were set deeply in the novel. Mary Shelley was often asked how she, then a young girl, came to think of, and to dilate upon, so very hideous an idea. 'I believe it was more than just an idea that came from a terrifying dream.' We have to remember that Mary, though young, had already lost a child, and was again pregnant with a second. Younger than twenty years, she was aware of the deepest fears and desires to do with creation.

We have mentioned the ancient creation myths. There are other deep fears too. These are also connected with fear of death. Central motifs of this novel are the themes of Fire and Ice. Ice and fire are opposites. They are closely connected to primitive bodily sensations. Ice is fixed and solid; fire is free and powerful. Again, there are connections with Prometheus and the theft of fire. Fire is a force that has exercised the minds and imaginations of people in all times, even in ancient times. Especially in ancient times, we could argue, because the nature and origins of fire were not fully understood. There seems to be an ancient and deep-seated fear of Fire, a force than can both warm and destroy, give pleasure and yet inflict pain.

The Monster is made for tragedy. He wants a mate, gets one, and loses her. In the end he despairs. Out of his despair comes a desire to die. He makes off for the cold regions of the North Pole. This is the land of ice. Yet the Monster plans a suicide by fire. 'I shall quit your vessel on the ice raft which brought me hither' he tells Walton. This is Mary Shelley tapping into another ancient myth, that of death and resurrection, like a Phoenix, rising anew from a funeral pyre.

All this might seem to be enough to explain the theme's potency. But other points need to be mentioned. By the C19, and certainly in twentieth century, the advances of medicine were many. Society seemed altogether a safer place. There was, in Europe at least, stable government. For many people life has become too safe. In such situations, not least when we are young, we seek thrills and fears. We pay money – and these days good money - to go on the Big Dipper at the seaside, or the Ghost Train at the funfair. We want to be terrified.

In 1818 people who read books sought their terror in the Gothic novels of Mrs Radcliffe. In Jane Austen's

Northanger Abbey, which is an accomplished satire on the Gothic novel, Henry Tilney talks of his hair standing on end after reading Mysteries of Udolpho. There was, therefore, a ready public for Mary Shelley's book. This explains its welcome and we have already analysed the reasons for its success. But not its lasting success. That is to be found in another element of the Gothic novels.

Along with the terror of dark castles and mysterious strangers, of dark happenings at dead of night, there is also a sexual fear. There is a fear of rape, and perhaps of even more unpleasant happenings in those strange corridors and secret rooms. Fear of rape is also an ancient fear. This also Mary Shelley tapped into most successfully. The Monster is roaming about at night. Anything fearful could happen. This is the power of the untamed, and the unnamed. We remember that Frankenstein was so horrified by his creation that he never gave it a name. It is always the Monster.

After rape, there comes a birth. There is in this novel a strong and powerful vein of woman's myth making. Mary Shelley's mother, Mary Wollstonecraft, 1797, Wollstonecraft gave birth to her second daughter, Mary. Although the delivery went well initially, the placenta broke during the birth and became infected; puerperal fever was more common in the C18 than it is nowadays. The mother did not die immediately. After several days of agony, Wollstonecraft died of septicaemia,

When such a tragedy occurs, the surviving child often experiences feelings of guilt. And when Godwin re-married, and the new step-mother favoured her own children (as is naturally to be expected) and Mary was left largely to her own devices, it was natural that her imagination would be fed, and fears that the child had killed the mother, the creator as it were, were strong.

These fears of infant murder of the parent – so richly explored by Sophocles in the Oedipus trilogy of plays - are the very fears evoked by the horror story. Mary Shelley is exploring the deepest emotions of women. Birth and death are fastened together. Mary lost children herself. This also helps to explain the novel's potency. Mary Shelley is referring to fears and anxieties about the creative process that had formerly been excluded from novels. Even today many people remain ignorant of the processes that bring about conception and birth. That ignorance was even stronger in past times.

So there is a feminine strand that helps to explain the novel's potency over two centuries. That should not surprise us, as the author was a woman with those very fears and anxieties.

The novel has been popular in the nonprint media of film and television. Few may now read the book, as few may have read it for many years, but the visual media have kept the tale to the forefront, and often added to it, gratuitously in many cases.

It is easy enough to explain the popularity of the novel in other media than print. Yet the elements of the story are those that explain its potency, and not anything intrinsic to the media of film or television. Yet cinema has allowed the myths embedded in the novel to be shared by millions all over the world who would never read the novel. The films are never as rhetorical and loftily mannered as the language of the novel. The language of the novel makes it inaccessible to millions. The film is the popular medium of our times. It also bridges the gap between popular and high culture.

It is true that in many films the novel has been changed. Yet the mythic elements remain, except in the attempts at comedy. Visualisation in all its forms is a powerful tool. So powerful indeed, that people have wished to give the Monster a name, and by some queer alchemy have called him 'Frankenstein.' 'As if in the popular imagination creator and created are one and the same person. The mad scientist becomes a Monster. The kind and scientific Dr Jekyll, as in R L Stevenson's story, becomes the horrific Mr Hyde. Good and evil reside in one person. We have a part of us that is light, another side that belongs to the night. It is to both sides of our nature - the good and the evil, the light and the dark, the scientific and the superstitious, the modern and the mythic, the conscious and the unconscious- that this novel powerfully appeals to those many sides of our human nature.

If you have only watched the movies, try the novel too; you may find it more accessible than you feared.

Elements of the Gothic

1. Setting.

The action takes place in and around an old castle or dilapidated mansion, sometimes abandoned, sometimes apparently occupied. The castle contains secret passages, trap doors, locked rooms, trick panels with hidden levers, dark or hidden staircases, and possibly ruined sections.

The castle may be near or connected to caves, which lend their own haunting flavour with their darkness, uneven floors, dark dank passages, claustrophobia, and mystery. These caves may be home to terrifying creatures such as monsters, or deviant forms of humans: vampires, zombies, werewolves, bats. Translated into the modern novel or filmmaking, the setting might be in an old house or mansion--or even a new house--where unusual camera angles, sustained close ups during movement, and darkness or shadows create the same sense of claustrophobia and entrapment. The house might be dark, because it has been abandoned, or it might at first seem light and airy, but when night comes and people turn off the lights, snuff out the candles, to go to bed, or at some dramatic point the lights fail because of a violent raging storm.

Darkness and the forbidding place serve to create a sense of unease and foreboding, contributing toward the atmospheric element of fear and dread. Darkness also allows sudden and frightening appearance of people, animals, or monsters.

2. An atmosphere of mystery and suspense.

The work, be it novel or movie, is pervaded by a threatening feeling, a fear enhanced by the unknown. This atmosphere is sometimes advanced when characters see only a glimpse of something. Was that a person rushing out the window or only the wind blowing a curtain? Was that a dead body or a figment of imagination? Is that creaking sound coming from someone's step on the squeaky floor, or only the normal sounds of the night? Often the plot itself is built around a mystery, such as unknown parentage, a disappearance, or some other inexplicable event. People disappear or show up dead inexplicably.

Someone arrives, a past acquaintance or colleague, and the news they impart add to the mix of suspicion and dread. One thinks of Mr Mason arriving unannounced at Thornfield Hall to see Edward Rochester in Charlotte Bronte's magisterial novel Jane Eyre.

In both novels and movies, and especially the latter, inexplicable events are often murders. The bodies are sometimes mutilated in ways that defy explanation-- 'What kind of monster could do this?' or 'Here's the body, but there's no blood.' When the corpses start to mount, suspense is raised as to who will get killed next. In filmmaking, the atmosphere can be created largely by the music. Anyone who has watched a horror movie with the sound off knows this.)

3. Ancient prophecy

This is connected with the castle or its inhabitants (either former or present). The prophecy is usually obscure, partial, or confusing.

4. Omens, portents, visions.

A character may have a disturbing dream or waking vision, or some phenomenon may be seen as a portent of coming events. For example, if a statue falls over inexplicably, it may portend a death. In modern fiction, a character might see something (a shadowy figure stabbing another shadowy figure) and think that it was a dream.

Sometimes an omen will be used for foreshadowing, while other writers will tweak the reader by denying expectation--what we thought was foreshadowed, was not.

5. Supernatural events.

Dramatic, amazing events occur, such as ghosts walking, or inanimate objects such as a suit of armour or a mysterious painting appear to come miraculously to life.

In some novels, such events are ultimately given a natural explanation, while in others the events are supernatural and that is how they must be accepted by the reader. As can be expected, knowing their modus operandi, Hollywood and Hammer and the like use special effects to a large degree to provide fire, earthquakes, moving statues, and so forth, often deliberately blurring the line between the human and natural, and modern special effects.

6. Overwrought emotions.

The narration may be highly sentimental, and the characters often overcome by anger, sorrow, surprise, and especially terror. Characters suffer from raw nerves and a feeling of impending doom. Crying and emotional speeches are frequent. Breathlessness and panic are common. In movies of the Gothic genre, screaming, by blond vulnerable women often, is common.

7. Women in distress.

This is a stock element, harking back to fears and fantasies of rape. As an appeal to the pathos and sympathy of the reader, the female characters often face events that leave them fainting, terrified, screaming, or weeping. A lonely and oppressed heroine is usually the central figure of the novel, so her sufferings are even more pronounced and the focus of the reader's attention. The women suffer all the more because they are often abandoned, left alone (either on purpose or by accident), and have no one to protect them.

8. Women threatened by a powerful male.

One or more male characters has the power, as king, lord of the manor, father, or guardian, to demand that a female character do something intolerable or immoral. The woman may be commanded to marry someone she does not love (it may even be the powerful male himself), or commit a crime. Failure to obey the command may be met with a threat of physical punishment or sexual violation.

9. The metonymy of gloom and horror.

Metonymy is the attribution of human feelings and responses to inanimate things or animals, used especially in art and literature. Metonymy is a subtype of metaphor, in which something (rain, for example) is used to stand for something else (like sorrow). The film and television industries like to use metonymy as a quick shorthand, so we often notice that it is raining in funeral scenes. This is, of course, a kind of device that John Ruskin called the pathetic fallacy

35

The following metonymies for doom and gloom all suggest some element of mystery, danger, or the supernatural:

Howling wind and sweeping rain;

Thunder and lightning;

The approach of footsteps in the dark;

Clanking chains and rusty door hinges creaking;

The howling of dogs or wolves;

Imprisonment in dark dank rooms;

Deranged laughter;

10. The vocabulary of the Gothic.

The constant use of the appropriate vocabulary set creates and sustains the atmosphere of the Gothic. Using the right words maintains the dark-and-stimulated feel that defines the Gothic. Here as an example are some of the words (in several categories) that help make up the vocabulary of the Gothic in The Castle of Otranto

Six Top Gothic Novels

1. The Castle of Otranto by Horace Walpole

Horace Walpole published the first gothic novel almost two and a half centuries ago. The Castle of Otranto (1765) created a confluence of medievalism and terror that struck readers as original.

2. Vathek by William Beckford

William Beckford's History of the Caliph Vathek (1786) merged the 18th century fashion for oriental tales with the newly-established gothic tradition.

3. The Mysteries of Udolpho by Ann Radcliffe

Radcliffe's 1794 work anticipates Stoker's ability to describe landscapes unseen by the author. She has a masterful ability to suggest the supernatural without ultimately invoking it.

4. The Monk by Matthew Lewis

One of the most vicious, rip-roaring and entertaining novels of the entire gothic genre.

5. Frankenstein by Mary Shelley

Together with John Polidori's The Vampire (the first fictional vampire tale), Frankenstein (1818) emerged from a wager at the Villa Diodati on the shores of Lake Geneva. It created a monster rivalled only by Count Dracula.

6. Dracula by Bram Stoker

A long and complex work, first published in 1897. Arguably the greatest, certainly the most popular gothic novel of them all.

www.ingramcontent.com/pod-product-compliance
Lightning Source LLC
Chambersburg PA
CBHW021121020426
42331CB00004B/578